STARTUPS

Aaron Erhardt
2020

DEDICATION

To Caleb Ashby and Keith Travis, my dear friends
and devoted co-workers.

INTRODUCTION

For Christians, encouragement is like oil to an engine. It is an essential lubricant that keeps everything running smoothly. It helps us stay cool and guards against harmful deposits that could wear us down. When that oil runs out, however, things start to grind and eventually the vehicle stalls.

"Encouragement" is more than giving someone a compliment or saying nice things to make them feel good about themselves. In the New Testament, it carries the idea of calling someone to your side in order to strengthen or motivate them to act in a certain way. It comforts and supports, but also challenges and exhorts. And it is something we all need "every day" (Hebrews 3:13).

This book is written to encourage. It is designed to lift you up and push you onward. Hopefully, each of the "spiritual startups" will provide some of the oil you'll need traveling down the highway of life. God bless you!

CONTENTS

HOME ALONE

If you have seen the holiday classic "Home Alone," you'll remember the dramatic scene when Kate McCallister suddenly realized her son had been left behind in Chicago. She was on a plane with her family mid-flight to France when an uneasy feeling arose that she had forgotten something. — Did they turn off the coffeemaker? Did they lock the door? Did they shut the garage? — She then leaned forward and screamed, "Kevin!" Kate was in agony for three long days before finally reuniting with her son. She was impressed to see that Kevin had handled himself quite nicely.

Mary could certainly relate to that story. She would have known exactly how Kate felt. In Luke 2, Mary and her family were "mid-flight" to Nazareth when she suddenly realized her son had been left behind in Jerusalem. She too was in agony for three long days before finally reuniting with her son. And like Kate, Mary was astonished at how well her son had handled himself. Both boys were just fine in their father's house!

HENRY "BOX" BROWN

Henry "Box" Brown was a 19th-century slave in Virginia. He devised a plan to escape slavery by having himself mailed to a free state by *Adams Express Company*, which was known for its confidential and efficient services. It cost him $86 dollars to be shipped in a small wooden crate (3 feet long by 2 feet wide) that was marked "dry goods." All he had was a single hole for air, a little water, and a few biscuits. Brown almost died along the way, but finally emerged 27 hours later in Pennsylvania.

Brown's plan required him to be placed in a confined space and carried by others for 27 hours to secure his freedom. God's plan required Jesus to be placed in a confined space, the womb of a woman, and carried by her for nine months to secure our freedom. Jesus was not being shipped from oppression; He was being shipped to oppression. He went from paradise to a plantation for our liberation!

BROKEN BEAUTY

"Kintsugi" is the Japanese art of repairing broken ceramics using lacquer mixed with gold, silver, or platinum. It sees breakage as something to be highlighted rather than hidden, and the end result often increases the object's value. Kintsugi makes the broken beautiful.

Kintsugi perfectly illustrates the Gospel. We are broken; God takes the pieces and puts them back together; and the end result is something more valuable and beautiful than before. Jesus Christ is the lacquer that makes this possible. However, before God can turn our mess into a masterpiece, we must come to grips with the fact that we are broken. Then and only then will God make the broken beautiful!

MARITAL BLISS

A little boy asked his mom why the girl at a wedding wears all white. His mom said, "The girl is called a 'bride,' and she wears white because it is the happiest day of her life." The boy then asked, "Why is the man dressed in all black?"

Many people view marriage like a hot bath — "once you get used to it, it's not so hot." To them, marriage is not a word but a sentence. As one man said, "Marriage is when a man loses his bachelor's degree and a woman gets her master's degree." The truth is, however, when done right marriage is a great blessing. It truly is a gift from God (Psalm 18:22).

YOUNG SOLIDER

During the 17th century, Oliver Cromwell, Lord Protector of England, sentenced a young soldier to be executed. It was to take place when the curfew bell sounded. However, the bell did not sound. The soldier's fiancé had climbed into the belfry and clung to the clapper of the bell to prevent it from striking. When she was summoned by Cromwell to account for her actions, she wept as she showed him her bruised and bleeding hands. Cromwell's heart was touched and he said, "Your lover shall live because of your sacrifice. Curfew shall not ring tonight!" Cromwell commuted the sentence.

All of us were like that young soldier. The guilt of our sin was exposed, and punishment was soon to commence. Then love intervened. It was not in the form of a girl climbing into the belfry and clinging to the clapper of the bell, but in the form of God's Son climbing down from heaven and clinging to the old rugged cross. Her bruising and bleeding were nothing compared to His. And just as the soldier was spared by her act of love, we are spared by His act of love. If I may slightly modify Cromwell's words, "We shall live because of His sacrifice!"

NO RIDING THE FENCE!

When Michael Jordan saw that his friend's closet was divided in half between Puma gear and Nike gear, he gathered up all the Puma gear and carried it into the living room. He then grabbed a butcher knife, cut it all up into pieces, and disposed of it in the dumpster. Jordan told his friend, "Don't ever let me see you in anything other than Nike. You can't ride the fence."

Too often the "closets of our hearts" are divided between competing interests. — God and money, God and self, God and work, God and sports, God and people. — When that happens, we need to rip out whatever is sharing space with the Lord and throw it away. We can't ride the fence!

MY NAME ON HIS CROSS

A carpenter in Jerusalem supported his family by making crosses for the Romans to use in crucifixions. His young son often worked with him in the shop. One day, his son came running in with panic on his face and said, "Dad, the preacher that we love so much just passed by carrying a cross." His dad was quite upset, for he really loved Jesus of Nazareth. His son added, "And it gets worse. They are about to crucify Him on a cross that I made." "I am sure  that is not true," the father replied. "There are many carpenter shops that make crosses for the Romans." The son began to cry as he said, "You don't understand, dad, I always sign my work when I am finished. I just saw my name on His cross."

I can relate with the terror that young boy must have felt, for in a very real sense it is my name on that cross. I made it with my sins and signed it with my guilt. When I close my eyes and envision Jesus being led to Calvary, I see my name on His cross!

POISON

A man went to his father and said, "Dad, I can't take it anymore, my wife is driving me insane! I want to kill her, but I'm afraid someone might find out I did it. Please help me." The father replied, "I can help you, but this is what you'll have to do. You're going to have to make amends with her so no one will suspect that it was you when she dies. Take very good care of her — be kind, grateful, patient, caring, less selfish, and help her with chores. Now, do you see this powder here? Just put a little in her food every day so she dies slowly."

After about thirty days, the son came back to his father and said, "I don't want her to die! I have come to love her. I now realize how wonderful we are together. How do I cut the effect of that poison?" The father answered, "Don't worry. What I gave you was rice powder. She's not going to die, because the poison was in you!"

STRONGER TOGETHER

There is a *Peanuts* cartoon where Lucy demands that Linus change the TV channel, threatening him with her fist if he doesn't. Linus asks, "What makes you think you can walk in here and take over?" Lucy says, "These five fingers. Individually they're nothing but when I curl them together like this, into a single unit, they form a weapon  that is terrible to behold." Linus then asks, "Which channel do you want?" And turning away, he looks down at his own fingers and says, "Why can't you guys get organized like that?"

When individual members in the local church come together and act as a single unit, we too form a weapon that is terrible to behold. We become an incredibly powerful instrument for God to use in the world. That's why the Scriptures talk so much about unity, and why Satan spends so much time trying to keep us apart.

FASTING FELINES

Daniel knew of the king's decree. It was clearly worded and widely circulated. It said that anyone caught praying to God for the next thirty days would be cast into a den of lions. Yet with his windows opened and his eyes closed, Daniel bowed his knees in prayer.

Daniel was convicted of violating the king's decree and thrown into the lion's den. However, God saved Daniel by putting the ferocious felines on a fast. He sent an angel to shut their mouths. Daniel was too committed to compromise his convictions, are we?

COOKIES

A young lady bought a book and some cookies while waiting for her flight. A man sat down next to her and began reading a magazine. The packet of cookies was on the armrest between them. When she ate the first cookie, he ate one also. She thought, "What nerve! I can't believe he would do that." This went on over and over. Each time she would take a cookie, he would grab one too. Finally, there was but one cookie left. Unbeliev-

ably, he took half of the last cookie. The lady was infuriated and stormed to the boarding place in a huff.

When the lady boarded the plane and sat down in her seat, she looked into her purse and saw her packet of cookies. It had not been touched. Feeling absolutely ashamed, she realized that the man had shared his cookies with her. May God help all of us develop a love for Him and others that demonstrates itself in our willingness to share the cookies!

NO REGRETS

When people are asked to name their greatest regrets in life, there is usually one word they all have in common — "not." Not speaking up, not spending more time, not asking for help, not chasing their dream, not leaving their comfort zone, not expressing their true feelings. Most people regret the times when they "didn't" do something. Times when opportunities were not seized, or chances were not taken, or resolutions were not kept.

Let's live today in such a way as to have no regrets tomorrow. Let's go "all in" and leave everything on the field. That means stepping out in faith and taking some risks, knowing that it is better to try and fail than to never try at all!

SINLESS SAVIOR

One of the most stunning statements made about Jesus in Scripture is this: He did not sin. He was a perfect person who never fell short, never missed the mark, never had a moral misstep or blameful blunder during His thirty-three years on earth. The Bible says He "knew no sin" (2 Corinthians 5:21), He was "without sin" (Hebrews 4:15), and He "committed no sin" (1 Peter 2:22).

That last verse is particularly powerful because of who wrote it. Peter was not only an apostle, he was part of the Lord's inner circle. He was with Jesus on a daily basis. There was probably no one who knew Him better or had greater access than Peter. Yet he says that Jesus committed no sin. There was no pride, prejudice, or pretense to be found. He never had a slip of the tongue or lapse in judgment. He was perfect! Therefore, Jesus is qualified to be our sacrifice for sin, "like that of a lamb without blemish or spot" (1 Peter 1:19).

IN OUR IMAGE

A teacher asked one of her students what he was drawing. The little boy answered, "I am drawing a picture of God." The teacher told the boy that he cannot draw a picture of God because no one knows what He looks like. The boy replied, "Well, they will when I am finished."

We all have our picture of what God looks like, don't we? This can be dangerous because we tend to envision Him in our own image, fitting neatly into a mode that we have developed. In other words, we confine God to our ways rather than conform ourselves to His ways. Be careful that your picture of God does not "draw" you away from the truth!

NO WORRIES

A woman picked up a glass of water and asked her audience, "How heavy is this?" Guesses ranged from 8 ounces to 20 ounces. The woman replied, "The actual weight does not matter. What matters is how long I hold it. If I hold it for a minute, it's not a problem. If I hold it for an hour, my arm will ache. If I hold it for a day, my arm will feel numb and even paralyzed." She continued, "And so it is with worry. If I worry for a little while, nothing seems to  happen. If I worry for a bit longer, I begin to hurt. If I worry all day long, I feel paralyzed and incapable of doing anything."

Jesus did not want His warriors to be worriers. He urged them to trust God, keep things in the proper perspective, and realize they do not have to carry their burdens alone. Moreover, research shows that 85% of what we worry about never happens. So, the best thing we can do is "let go and let God." Pass that glass!

FEELING EMPTY

D o you have a "void" inside that can't seem to be filled? Most of us do. But here's the irony, the more we try to fill that void, the emptier it becomes. For instance, if we try to fill it with food, we're left feeling hungry; if we try to fill it with people, we're left feeling lonely; if we try to fill it with money, we're left feeling bankrupt; if we try to fill it with entertainment, we're left feeling bored. These things may provide temporary relief, but they offer no permanent solution.

To truly find that which can make us full, we must look to that which is empty. "Some of our men went to the tomb and found it empty…" (Luke 24:24, GW). The empty tomb of Jesus Christ holds the answer to being made full.

SHARK BAIT

A marine biologist placed a shark in a tank with bait fish. The shark quickly swam around and ate all of them. The biologist then inserted a piece of clear fiberglass into the tank, creating two separate sections. When more bait fish were put in the other side, the shark quickly attacked but hit the divider and bounced off. Over time the shark got less aggressive and  finally gave up altogether. When the fiberglass was removed, the shark did not attack the bait fish swimming around because he still believed the barrier existed.

Some Christians are like that shark. They have been so discouraged by past setbacks that they stop trying and just give up. They convince themselves that barriers are always standing in the way, even when they aren't. However, Jesus taught His followers to be persistent and not to lose heart. Both sharks and saints would do well to remember the old proverb, "If at first you don't succeed, try, try again!"

JESUS SPOKE

Jesus did not pen a single page of the New Testament. He was not a writer, but a speaker. And He spoke like none other. His words left crowds stunned, critics silenced, cruelty stifled, and creation shaken. They were both piercing and powerful.

Jesus spoke and the sea stood still; Jesus spoke and the demon stood down; Jesus spoke and the deceased stood up; Jesus spoke and the disabled stood tall; Jesus spoke and the detractor stood corrected; Jesus spoke and the sinner stood forgiven. We speak because He spoke!

PERFECT GIFT

A man was crossing the desert and found a wonderful spring filled with cold water. It was so refreshing that he filled a leather bottle and took some to his king. Unaware that the water had been tainted by the container, he presented it to his lord. The king took a deep drink and then highly commended his loyal subject for the gift.

It was not the water the king enjoyed, but the love that motivated the man to bring it.

Like that king, our God is gracious and kind. He looks beyond the imperfection of the gifts we offer to the love that motivated those gifts in the first place. Such love makes bitter water better!

CRUCIFIXION

Jesus gave up magnificence for mundane, harmony for hatred, reverence for revulsion, and loftiness for lashings. He left His throne for thorns, His nobility for nails, and His crown for a cross.

Crucifixion was a particularly prolonged, painful, and public way to die. In fact, the word "excruciating" means "out of crucifying." The person usually lingered for hours before finally succumbing to heart failure, shock, asphyxia, or dehydration. The ISBE says, "The victim of crucifixion literally died a thousand deaths." And yet Jesus willingly took up His cross for us. Are we willing to take up our crosses for Him?

THE ROCK

When Andrew introduced his brother Simon to Jesus, the Lord looked at him intently and said, "You shall be called Cephas," or Peter ("rock"). Have you ever wondered why Jesus changed Simon's name? It had nothing to do with his physical appearance or the conversation that took place later at Caesarea Philippi. It had everything to do with the potential Jesus saw in him. He looked beyond what Simon was to what Simon could become.

Reaching Simon's potential was not easy. He made plenty of mistakes. There was the reckless rebuke (Matthew 16:21-23), the presumptuous proposal (Matthew 17:1-5), the selfish sleeping (Matthew 26:40-44), the detestable denials (Matthew 26:69-75), etc. However, he finally lived up to his new name and became a "rock" for the Lord. So, what does the Lord see in you?

BARABBAS

"Barabbas" was a notorious criminal who is mentioned in all four gospel accounts. Known by some manuscripts as "Jesus Barabbas," he had committed robbery and murder during an insurrection. And, as a result, he was an inmate on death row in Jerusalem at the time Jesus was brought before Pilate.

Pilate unwittingly pitted against each other two people who represented the most antagonistic forces of all time when he asked the crowd, "Whom do you want me to release for you: Barabbas, or Jesus who is called Christ?" Barabbas was the essence of carnality. He was a vile and violent lawbreaker. He was the worst Pilate could offer. Jesus, on the other hand, was the sinless Savior. He was the best God could offer. The contrast could not be clearer. Yet the crowd called for Barabbas to be released. They wanted him "let loose" (GNV). — The sad reality is that we "let Barabbas loose" every time we turn away from righteousness to pursue some sinful enticement. We are choosing carnality over Christ!

JUST BEYOND

A young girl lived near a spooky-looking cemetery, and in order to get to the store she had to follow a path that went through the cemetery. Yet the young girl never seemed to be afraid, even when it was dark outside. When someone asked her, "Aren't you scared walking through that cemetery?" she replied, "Oh, no, I am not scared, for my home is just beyond."

Because Jesus Christ was raised from the dead, Christians believe they have a home just beyond the cemetery and therefore have no need to fear it. Since He conquered death and lives again, they will also conquer death and live again.

GIANT SLAYER

David's "giant" stood over 9 feet tall, wearing body armor that weighed 125 pounds, and carrying a spear with a head that weighed 15 pounds. He was a champion warrior whose thundering voice and towering presence caused his enemies to fear. David did not appear to

 stand a chance. His opponent had all the advantages (size, experience, artillery, athleticism). However, David was not fighting alone. God was on his side.

Rather than looking at the size of the giant, David was looking at the size of his God. And as a result, he prevailed! The "giant" challenging you might come in the form of anger, anxiety, guilt, pride, or prejudice. It might be a financial burden or health crisis. However, God is bigger than that giant. He can help you to prevail!

DEFENSE LAWYER

There is an attorney who is willing to plead your case before the high court. He is a flawless and famed advocate for those who stand accused. You can rest easy with him on your side.

This attorney wants to stand up for you. He desires to be your defender. He is your one and only hope. And best of all, His services are offered free of charge. Do not miss your opportunity to get this "high-powered defense lawyer" on your side (1 John 2:1, Voice)!

WORTH

A man was speaking to about 200 people during a seminar. He held up a $20 bill and asked, "Who wants this?" Everyone's hand immediately went up in the air. He then crumpled up the $20 bill and asked, "Who wants this now?" The hands remained in the air. He proceeded to drop the $20 bill on the ground and grind it with his shoe as he asked, "How about now?" Still the room was full of raised hands. That is because the crumpled and dirty $20 bill had not lost its value. It was still worth something. And so it is with us!

There are times when sin leaves us crumpled and dirty. We are no longer "finely creased." However, that does not mean we have lost our value to God. He still sees worth in us, even at our most unworthy point. This does not excuse the need for repentance, but it should motivate us to seek repentance. God still wants us!

BUILD IT RIGHT

A wealthy businessman noticed that a local carpenter was living in a rundown house in the community. Therefore, he hired the carpenter to do some work for him while he went on a long vacation. He said, "I want you to build a house. Use only the best materials. Hire the best craftsmen. Spare no expense." However, the carpenter cut corners at every turn. He used inferior materials and sent unskilled workers to the site. When the rich man returned, he inspected the new house and then said, "Here are your keys." The carpenter had been building his own house!

This story should serve as a warning for all Christians. The cheating we do when no one else is looking affects us far more than we realize. Moral missteps and spiritual shortcuts now will lead to chipping, cracking, and even crumbling later. Don't look back on what you were building with regret!

SENSELESS STRIFE

A knight appeared before his king and declared, "Sire, I have just returned from pillaging and plundering all of your enemies to the east!" The king replied, "But I don't have any enemies to the east." The knight said, "You do now."

Too often Christians fight battles and make enemies that are not necessary. We "major in minors" and bind our traditions, preferences, and opinions as if they were Scripture. When that happens, the gospel is hindered and brethren are harmed. — Let us get with each other at the cross rather than getting cross with each other!

SACRIFICIAL LAMB

A man was working on the roof of a church building in Werden, Germany, when his safety belt snapped and he fell. The situation could have been tragic for the man if he had not landed on a lamb grazing below. Though the lamb died, the man survived. As a token of his appreciation, the man erected a stone carving of a lamb on the roof.

That lamb did not have a choice. He had no idea what was coming. If he had, there is no doubt the lamb would have moved over and let the man fall to his death. Yet there was another lamb that did have a choice. He did know what was coming. And by grace, He willingly chose to lay down His life for us!

FIRST FAMILY

Can you imagine being part of the "First Family" in America or the "Royal Family" in England? You would experience privileges that the rest of us can only dream about. For instance, you would have direct access to a very powerful person, be lavished with gifts that someone else paid for, be constantly protected from harm, and forever be recognized as belonging to an exclusive fraternity.

If you think that would be cool, this will really blow your mind. Christians have been adopted into the family of God. They are part of His household. He is their Father and Jesus is their older brother. They have become heirs of God and fellow heirs with Christ. As a result, Christians have direct access to a very powerful person, are lavished with gifts that someone else paid for, are constantly protected from harm, and will forever be recognized as belonging to an exclusive fraternity. So, are you up for adoption?

RASHNESS

A group of men were looking for a place to hunt. They pulled into a farmer's driveway and one of them went up to see if they could hunt on the land. The farmer said, "You can hunt, but do me a favor. That donkey over there is 20 years old and is very sick. I just don't have the heart to kill her. Will you do it for me?" The man replied, "Of course I will." As he got back in the car, the man decided to play a joke on his friends. He said, "We can't hunt here, but I'm going to teach that old man a lesson he won't forget." He then stuck his gun out the window and shot the donkey. Almost immediately, a second shot rang out from the passenger side as one of his friends yelled, "I got the cow!"

"Rashness" is being overhasty in action without due consideration. There are many examples of rashness in the Bible. For instance, Moses acted rashly getting water from the rock and was prohibited from entering the Promised Land (Numbers 20); and Jephthah and Herod made rash vows that cost people their lives (Judges 11; Mark 6). Rashness can hurt feelings, ruin friendships, and divide congregations. It is far better to practice prudence. As Proverbs says, "Wise people think before they act..." (13:16, NLT).

CHILEAN MINERS

On August 5, 2010, a group of 33 Chilean miners became trapped nearly half a mile beneath the surface of the earth. They found themselves cut off from above, buried 2,300 feet deep, and unable to do anything about it on their own. They had to rely on outside inter-

vention, which finally presented itself after 69 days in the form of a specially-designed capsule.

The rescue of the Chilean miners perfectly illustrates the concept of salvation by grace. Man is cut off from above, buried deep in sin, and unable to do anything about it on his own. He must rely on outside intervention, which has come in the form of Jesus Christ. He is the saving capsule! However, man must get "into" Him (Galatians 3:27) and "remain" there (John 15:4) to reach the top.

ROYAL PROTOCOL

Lebron James violated royal protocol by wrapping his arm around Duchess Kate for a picture in 2014. The faux pas took place at an NBA game between the Cavaliers and Nets in New York, and it left the British media reeling. Though palace officials downplayed the incident, royals are to initiate handshakes and conversations, and they are not to be touched.

I wonder if Christians sometimes view God like that. In their desire to show Him proper respect and reverence, they keep their distance for fear of violating some kind of "royal protocol." They don't want to get too close or speak too soon. While it is true that God is holy and must be approached with the utmost regard, He is also

our "Father" and we are His "children." Our relationship is more familial than formal. He loves us and seeks our affection!

RESTRAINED BY LOVE

A three-year-old boy was sitting at the dinner table with his parents when he suddenly declared, "Jesus died on the cross." They were impressed by his surprising remark and asked him why Jesus died on the cross. He thought about it for a minute and said, "Because He couldn't get off." There is actually a lot of truth to that answer. Jesus couldn't get off the cross — not because of

the nails in His hands and feet, but because of His love for mankind. That love held Him far more firmly than any physical restraints ever could.

Jesus gave up magnificence for mundane, harmony for hatred, reverence for revulsion, and loftiness for lashings. He left His throne for thorns, His nobility for nails, and His crown for a cross.

He did for us what we could not have done for ourselves. As Peter wrote, "Christ also suffered once for sins, the righteous for the unrighteous, that He might bring us to God" (1 Peter 3:18).

THE EXTRA MILE

Have you ever had somebody go out of their way for you? I am not talking about in little ways, like getting up from the table to grab the ketchup; I mean in ways that really required effort and sacrifice.

Not long ago my family was driving down I-65 when our tire blew. It was a cold, snowy night. We didn't have cell phone reception or much distance between us and the passing semi-trucks. Feeling desperate, we sent a text to someone who lived in the area. He soon arrived at our stranded vehicle on the side of the road. He then drove us to get a new tire at Wal-Mart, bought us dinner, took us back to the car, and gladly installed the new tire. He went the extra mile at his own time and expense, much like the Samaritan man in the story Jesus once told (Luke 10:30-36). — I guess we could call him "The Good Kentuckian!"

DYNAMITE

The gospel is "the power of God" (Romans 1:16). "Power" comes from the Greek word *dynamis,* from which we get our English word dynamite. Hence, the gospel is God's dynamite! And we certainly see that dynamite working in the lives of Christians around the world.

Christians have seen the gospel "blow up" their fears and failures and give them a true sense of peace. They have received a "blast" of purpose in life; they have obtained a "burst" of understanding in the Word; and they have experienced an "explosion" of improvement in the home. That same gospel can give your life the "boom" it so desperately needs!

LEGALISM

Prior to WWII, France developed a line of defensive fortifications along its eastern border called the "Maginot Line." It consisted of concrete bunkers and weapon installations that were designed to thwart any frontal assault by the Germans. When that time came, however, the Maginot Line proved to be unsuccessful, because most of Hitler's forces bypassed the line and invaded instead through the north, which the allied forces were not anticipating. As a result, France fell in about six weeks.

Many of our churches today are digging in against the threat of liberalism, and rightfully so. Basic moral values are under attack, the integrity of the Bible is being challenged, and everything from the role of women to the authority of elders is being reinterpreted. However, while we build our defensive fortifications against that threat, we need to be on guard against another possible invasion which is less anticipated but certainly as dangerous — legalism. Legalism binds where God has not bound and forbids what is allowed. So, let us beware of those who would slip in to take our liberty!

GOD KNEW

God knew what awaited His Son. He knew they would spit in His face, strike Him on the head, strip off His clothes, and sarcastically kneel before Him. He knew that His Son would be scourged, spiked, and speared. None of it was a surprise. All of it was expected. From the stumbling Savior trying to carry His own cross, to the scoffing soldiers casting lots for His garments, to the sobbing

sisters watching in the distance, this horror scene had played out in God's mind many times. And yet He allowed it to happen.

God's love is too great to describe with words. It is beyond the limits of human language. He "did not spare His own Son but gave Him up for us all" (Romans 8:32). What earthly father would give up his son for someone else? Yet God did just that.

ADOPTED BY GOD

"Adoption" comes from a compound Greek word that means "to place as son." Though adoption was not widely practiced among the Jews, it was quite prevalent in the Roman Empire. An adopted son was deliberately chosen to perpetuate the father's name and to inherit his estate. Paul said that Christians have been adopted into the family of God.

Jesus is the only natural son of God. The rest of us are sons by adoption. We have become His children and He is our "Abba." ("Abba" is an informal Aramaic word for "father." It is a term of endearment reserved for a child. The English equivalent is "daddy" or "papa.") This makes us heirs of God and fellow heirs with Jesus.

HUMILITY

Two Soviet ships collided in the Black Sea off the coast of Russia in 1986, killing many people. An investigation revealed that the crash was not caused by mechanical failure or weather conditions. It was the result of pride. Both captains knew of the other ship's presence and could have easily steered clear, but neither would yield. A lack of humility cost hundreds of people their lives.

Everything about the Lord's life — from His birth in a barn to His burial in a borrowed tomb — stood as a

rebuke of pride. He was meek, mild, and modest. He sought to serve rather than be served. He understood that God reigns in the highest heavens and in the lowliest hearts. The poor in spirit will be rich in spirit!

THERE WERE WITNESSES

Suppose a man robbed a bank at gunpoint, and five people got a good look at him. Their eyewitness testimony would carry a lot of weight in court, wouldn't it? Now suppose that five more people came forward who also got a good look at the man, and then five more people after that. Can you  imagine how overwhelming the testimony of 15 eyewitnesses would be in the conviction of that criminal?

Now consider how many people were eyewitnesses to the resurrection of Jesus Christ. There weren't just 5 or 10 or 15, we're talking about more than 500 people. And they all got a good look at Him! There was Mary Magdalene and the other women, the apostle Peter, the two disciples on the road to Emmaus, the rest of the apostles, the five hundred, James, Stephen, and Paul. Hence, there is no question that Jesus Christ was raised from the dead. The eyewitness testimony is simply overwhelming. The only question is whether you will make Him the Lord of your life.

GAZE OF GRACE

When the Israelites despised the food that God sent them from heaven, He sent them something from the earth — fiery serpents. "Fiery" could have reference to their color, but more likely refers to their venom. Their bite burned! The NIV says "venomous snakes" and the NRSV says "poisonous serpents." These agents of death were coming out of crevices, curled up in corners, slithering in the sand, and hissing at their heels. They spread through the camp like wildfire and killed many of

the Israelites. However, when the people begged for mercy, a bronze serpent was lifted up that they could look upon and be healed.

The Israelites experienced a horror scene that sounds like something out of Hollywood: slithering slayers lurking in the shadows, hiding behind rocks, climbing on the pottery, and clinging to the walls, just waiting to attack their next victim. Then grace entered the picture. God intervened. Healing happened. The symbol of death became a symbol of life. All they had to do was "look" to the right thing in obedient faith. Have you done that?

THE GREAT RAID

"The Great Raid" was a daring rescue of over 500 POWs from a Japanese prison camp in the Philippines just before they were to be executed. A group of Army Rangers and Scouts slipped 35 miles behind enemy lines and staged a devastating assault under the cover of darkness, killing all the Japanese guards without harming any of the POWs.

The POWs had been held captive for 3 long years. They were beaten, forced to do hard labor, required to stand at attention for hours, and lived on less than a handful of rice per day. Yet because of the courageous acts of others, they were freed. They were liberated from their confinement! Sound familiar? We were being held captive in Satan's prison camp doomed to die until someone courageously slipped across enemy lines to free us. Jesus Christ put His own life on the line to save ours!

WINE SHORTAGE

A wine shortage may not sound like a big deal today, but in the first century it was a huge issue. The groom's family was responsible for the refreshments, and to run out of wine during the festivities was socially dis-

graceful. It would bring the family a lot of shame and embarrassment, and they could even be subject to a fine.

Jesus did not have to save the day. It was not His party or His problem. Yet He knew that a family's reputation was at stake. He knew that the newly-weds happy affair was in danger of a cultural catastrophe. Therefore, Jesus did what seemed impossible. He turned large jars of water into wine. That's grace. And it was the best-tasting wine ever! More grace.

COMPASSION

A man forgot to silence his phone before service started and it rang during a prayer. The preacher scolded him, several members made condescending remarks, and his wife lectured him on the way home for being so careless. You could see the shame on his face, and the man never went back to church again.

That evening, the man went to a local bar. His nerves were shot from the earlier incident at church and he accidentally spilled his drink on the table. The waiter apologized and gave him a napkin to clean himself. Another man came over smiling and wiped the floor. The manag-

er then offered him a complimentary drink and said, "Don't worry about that? We all make mistakes." The man has been going back to that bar ever since. — Isn't it sad when the world shows more compassion than Christians?

BOOTS

A kindergarten teacher was helping one of her students put on his boots. She pulled and tugged until they were finally on his feet. The boy said, "Teacher, they're on the wrong feet." She almost whimpered as she struggled to get the boots off and back on the right feet. Then the boy announced, "These aren't my boots." She bit her tongue rather than scream, "Why didn't you say so earlier?" Once the boots were off, the boy added, "They're my brother's boots. My mom made me wear them." The teacher didn't know whether to laugh or cry. She finally mustered up the grace to wrestle the boots on his feet again. "Now, where are your gloves?" she asked. "I stuffed them in my boots," he replied.

"Patience" comes from a Greek word that means "long-tempered." It is the opposite of being short-tempered. It is the ability to stay calm when provoked and to endure injury without retaliating. A.T. Robertson said it means "holding out a long time and putting up with a great deal." Patience is a quality of God that should characterize His children. Remember that when the boot won't scoot!

FOR US

The sacrifice of Christ did not begin on the cross, or in the garden, or in the manger. It began in heaven when He laid aside His glory and consented to come to earth. He left the abode of God for the abode of man and exchanged exaltation for humiliation, magnitude for servitude, a radiant crown for a rugged cross, and a hallowed throne for a hollowed tomb. And it was all for us!

Jesus did not have to do it. He chose to do it. His great sacrifice, which started in heaven and culminated on the cross, brought hope to the hopeless and life to the lifeless. It did for us what we could not have done for ourselves.

SPECIAL DELIVERY

Jesus gave up worship for a womb, majesty for a manger, splendor for a stable, and heaven for a hamlet. He went from being wrapped in glory to being wrapped in strips of cloth. He left the breathtaking for breath-taking. The Infinite became an infant. And He did it for us!

It is incredible to know that the baby Mary delivered had actually come to deliver her and everyone else. He was born so we could be born again. He lived on earth so we could live in heaven. That helpless infant lying in the manger had come to help the truly helpless.

LIFELINE

Arland Williams was a passenger on *Air Florida Flight 90*, which crashed into freezing waters in the middle of a snowstorm. When a rescue helicopter arrived and threw him a lifeline, he immediately gave it to another passenger. When the helicopter came back, Arland did the same thing again and again. When the helicopter returned a final time, Arland was dead. He had used his

last ounce of energy to save a stranger.

We were like those passengers stranded in the freezing waters. The storm of sin had brought us down, and the only thing colder than the crippling current was the realization that death was rapidly approaching and there was nothing we could do about it. But just then, in the midst of our hopeless despair, a lifeline was tossed in our direction by a fellow passenger. He was willing to save our lives even when it meant losing His own.

THE PRODIGAL

The prodigal son did not deserve a party. A lashing, maybe. A lecture, certainly. But not a party. His reckless behavior was simply inexcusable. After all, how dare he demand his part of the inheritance while his father still lived? How dare he go off and blow the money on loose living in a foreign country? How dare he come back now with nothing to show for himself? He deserved banishment, not a banquet! He should be sentenced, not celebrated! But that's the point. God is willing to extend

grace to even the worst sinners when they seek it. It is not based on their merit, but on His mercy.

The father could have put his son on some sort of probation. That alone would have been more than he deserved and a remarkable demonstration of grace. But probation never crossed his mind. He immediately issued a full pardon!

THE GOLDEN TEXT

John 3:16 is probably the most popular passage in the Bible. Commonly called "The Golden Text," it appears on bracelets, banners, billboards, backpacks, and bumper stickers. When Tim Tebow wore "John 3:16" on his eye black during the 2009 Championship Game, over 92 million people looked that verse up on *Google*.

John 3:16 begins with God and ends with eternal life. Nestled between love and Son is the world. Belief is the condition attached, though it includes obedience (vv. 21, 36). The bridge between God and the world is love. The bridge between Son and eternal life is belief. What an amazing word picture!

HEALING PLACE

Jesus never used the word "grace," yet no one has ever defined it better. He was grace personified. He was a walking, talking, living manifestation of God's unmerited favor bestowed on an unworthy world. He was a place of refuge for the weary, teary, and leery.

This is not to say that Jesus overlooked or tolerated sin, but He first showed compassion. He knew that you had to love people before you could lead them and extended an open hand rather than a pointing finger. That is why the sad, sick, sinful, and struggling were drawn to Him. They saw Jesus as the ultimate "healing place." *People do not care how much you know until they know how much you care!*

NOT SO AMAZING

I fear that some Christians take grace for granted because they consider themselves to be pretty good people already. Before their conversion, they worked hard and stayed out of trouble. They were caring, sharing, and rarely swearing. Their version of John Newton's classic hymn on grace would be, "Amazing grace how sweet the sound that saved a decent person like me."

Before Christians can truly be shaped, softened, strengthened, and sustained by grace, they must learn to appreciate just how bad things were for them. They must come to grips with the fact that they were as helpless and hopeless as everybody else.

OBSCURITY

The most significant event in human history up to that point, the birth of Christ, unfolded in a seemingly insignificant fashion: an obscure cave, in an obscure village, to obscure people, at an obscure time. There was no pomp or pageantry. There was no celebration in the streets. There was no media trying to catch a glimpse of the new king. The enormity was couched in obscurity.

While the birth of Christ certainly garnered all of heaven's attention (Luke 2:13-14), few on earth seemed to notice. Yet in a wonderful display of grace, the Creator took part in creation. God became a man. Messiah arrived. Bethlehem, which means "house of bread," brought forth the Bread of Life (John 6). How fitting!

FOREMOST SINNER

Jeffrey Dahmer was one of the most notorious serial killers in American history. He was sentenced to 15 consecutive life terms for the rape, murder, and dismemberment of 17 males between 1978 and 1991. Some of

the murders involved cannibalism. Yet he learned the truth and was baptized into Christ shortly before he was beaten to death on November 28, 1994.

If Paul was the "foremost" sinner of the first century, Jeffrey Dahmer was certainly among the "foremost" sinners of the twentieth century. Yet neither man was beyond the scope of God's grace. His grace was greater than their disgrace!

GOOD NEWS

An unplanned pregnancy followed by an unpleasant pilgrimage to an overpopulated peasant village just in time to give birth doesn't exactly sound like good news, especially when the delivery room was a cave and a feeding trough served as a crib. But it was good news!

What heaven could not contain, a body did. God dwelled within the womb of a woman. He was fashioned in flesh and inhabited humanity. The Son of God became the Son of man. Praise God for His wonderful wisdom!

WHAT A GIFT!

Jesus was rich but became poor so we who were poor could become rich. Isn't that an amazing thought? He chose to walk the dusty streets of earth so we could walk the golden streets of heaven; to wear a crown of thorns on His head so we could wear a crown of righteousness on our head; to die physically so we could live spiritually. His grace was our gain!

Jesus did not owe us anything. There was nothing we had done to deserve or earn His favor. It was the result of mercy, not merit. He did for us what we could not have done for ourselves.

LAZY BONES

"Sloth" is laziness. It can denote either inactivity or sluggishness in the performance of a task. Words like "apathy," "idleness," "indifference," and "lethargy" are often associated with sloth. A slothful person delays work and does not complete work already begun. He lives by

the saying, "Never do today what you can put off till tomorrow." He cuts corners and looks for the easy way out.

The slothful person — or "lazy bones" (NRSV) — is an aggravating (Proverbs 10:26), unmotivated (Proverbs 19:24), excuse-filled (Proverbs 22:13), self-conceited (Proverbs 26:16) drain on society. He is a disgrace to himself and his Creator. He will rust out long before he will wear out!

BY GRACE

As Paul added his name to the list of post-resurrection appearances in 1 Corinthians 15, he expressed how unworthy he was to be an apostle. Then he added, "But by the grace of God I am what I am" (v. 10a). That is one of my favorite statements in the Bible.

Paul went from sinner to saint. He went from persecutor to preacher. He went from apostate to apostle. And it was all by grace! God bestowed favor on the one who deserved it the least. It was unearned and unmerited. But isn't that true of us all? Who among us deserves to be where we are? Who among us deserves the many blessings and benefits we enjoy in Christ? From the transgressions in our past to the treasures in our future, we too can say "by the grace of God I am what I am!"

SELF-CONTROL

Aristotle once said, "I count him braver who overcomes his desires than him who conquers his enemies; for the hardest victory is over self." His thoughts are very similar to those of Solomon, who said "he who rules his spirit" is better than "he who takes a city" (Proverbs 16:32).

"Self-control" is the restraint of passions and impulses. It refers to one who masters his appetites, emotions, inclinations, and urges. It involves not only abstinence from that which is prohibited, but moderation in that which is permissible. This elusive characteristic is absolutely essential, for if you do not conquer self it will conquer you!

THE GOLDEN RULE

Few passages are more recognizable than Matthew 7:12. It falls into the same category as Joshua 24:15 and John 3:16 in terms of familiarity. It is, of course, the golden rule. The golden rule says that we are to treat others the way we want to be treated. It is but another way of stating the command to "love your neighbor as yourself" (Matthew 22:39; Romans 13:9). Sadly, however, few people actually live by the golden rule.

The one who lives by the golden rule will not determine his treatment of others by asking what they deserve, but by asking how he would want to be treated in the same situation. He will seek the best for someone who may not seek the best for him.

LITTLE LAMB

I wonder how Mary must have felt on the long trip from Nazareth to Bethlehem. After all, it was about an 80-mile journey over bumpy and hilly terrain, she was riding on a donkey, and she was pregnant. Nine months pregnant! It is not as if Mary was reclining comfortably in a cushioned seat of a spacious SUV, with temperature control and high-performance tires. She was atop a rough-riding, slow-moving, fierce-smelling animal.

Then, as if the arduous journey were not enough, when Mary and Joseph finally reached their destination there was no place to stay. The town was packed with people, and the inn was full. Therefore, they had to take up lodging where the animals were kept. And it was there, in the most-humble of circumstances, that Mary had a little lamb!

RESET BUTTON

M any people are haunted by their past messes, mis-haps, and mistakes. Their former failures leave them with a feeling of emptiness and hopelessness. They hold them back and keep them down. If only there was a reset button for their life.

I have good news! A reset button exists in the form of Jesus Christ. He can erase your past and redirect your future. He can use the stumbling blocks of yesterday as stepping-stones for tomorrow. He can turn "IMPOSSI-BLE" into "I'M POSSIBLE."

THE LIGHTHOUSE

A battleship was at sea one night when the captain learned of another ship in the distance. He immediately had his signalman send a message, "We are on a collision course; advise you change course 20 degrees." A signal came back saying, "Advisable for you to change course 20 degrees." The captain sent another message, "I'm a captain; change course 20 degrees." "I am a seaman second class," came the reply. "You had better change course 20 degrees." By that time the captain was furious. He responded, "I'm a battleship; change course 20 degrees." Back came the flashing light, "I'm a lighthouse." The captain changed course.

The captain is like many people before their conversion. They are big in their own minds — full of pride, power, and prominence. They are a formidable force not to be reckoned with. Then they come in contact with the lighthouse, God Himself, and suddenly see the need to change course.

THE FIRST CHAIR

Thirteen crew members who had been taken captive by the North Koreans in 1968 were placed in a room together. After several hours, the door flung open and a guard brutally beat the man in the first chair with the butt of his rifle. The next day, as each man sat in his assigned place, the door again flung open and the man in the first chair was brutally beaten. On the third day, it had happened yet again.

Realizing that the man in the first chair would be beaten to death, another crew member took his place. For weeks, a new man stepped forward each day to sit in the horrible chair, knowing what would happen. To a much greater degree, Jesus stepped forward to suffer for us. He didn't sit in the first chair, but He did hang on the middle cross. And His pain was our gain!

STRENGTH IN WEAKNESS

God's strength is often demonstrated in weakness. For instance, He used seemingly insignificant creatures, like frogs and flies, to deliver the Israelites from Egyptian bondage; He used seemingly insignificant acts, like shouting and marching, to bring down the walls of Jericho; and He used seemingly insignificant men, like  fishermen and tax collectors, to spread the gospel around the world.

God made sure Gideon's army had few men and munitions before defeating the Midianites. This was to show them that He was the source of their victory. His strength was demonstrated in their weakness. And so it is today. We should never get too big in our own minds or lose sight of the fact that our victories come from God's greatness, not our own.

SNAKEBITE

When the devil commandeered a snake and tempted Eve in Genesis 3, he used some tricky tactics. For instance, he focused on God's restrictions (v. 1), he removed the threat of punishment (v. 4), he questioned God's motives (v. 5), and he attacked when the tree was visible (v. 6). Moreover, he went to the woman rather than the man, for God had given the command to Adam before Eve was created (Genesis 2:16).

Snakes would not have been feared by humans before the fall, so everything seemed harmless. Yet Adam and Eve bit off more than they could chew. And, truthfully, not much has changed. People are still quick to follow every "snake" that comes along and reject what God has said. However, the good news is that Jesus Christ has the "anti-venom." He can reverse the curse!

UPLIFTING

Jesus Garcia was a railroad brakeman in Mexico. On November 7, 1907, he noticed that some hay on the roof of a boxcar containing dynamite had caught fire. He drove the train at full-steam out of the town before the dynamite exploded, killing him but sparing many people. He is now revered as a national hero.

The self-sacrifice of Jesus Garcia is admirable and praiseworthy. He willingly gave himself to save others. However, no story of self-sacrifice in the history of the world is more impressive than that of another Jesus. Jesus Christ determined before the foundation of the world to leave the glories of heaven and give Himself as a sacrifice for "everyone" (Hebrews 2:9). He was "lifted up" to lift us up!

LET'S FACE IT

When Thomas Jefferson was President, he and a group of travelers were crossing a river that had overflowed its banks. Each man crossed on horseback struggling for his life. A lone traveler watched the group intently. He then asked Jefferson to take him across, which Jefferson did without hesitation. Once they safely reached the other side, somebody asked, "Why did you select the President for this favor?" The man was shocked to hear that it was the President who helped him across. He replied, "All I know is that on some of your faces was written the answer 'no,' and on some of your faces was written the answer 'yes.' His was a 'yes' face."

One of the most important decisions we make each day has to do with our attitude. As Christians, we need to make sure that our attitude is attractable. It should be warm and welcoming to others. — Our mood should mirror our message, our demeanor should depict our devotion, and our character should compliment our calling. — And rest assured, it will be written on our face!

THE GOOD SAMARITAN

The Good Samaritan went out of his way to help someone who probably would not have helped him, sacrificing his time and money. This is especially impressive when one considers the great animosity that existed between Jews and Samaritans. Jews considered Samaritans to be half-breeds cursed by God. There was even a saying among Jews, "It is better to take food from the mouth of a dog than from the hand of a Samaritan." The animosity was so strong that many Jews would go out  of their way to avoid Samaritan territory. And for most Samaritans, the feeling was mutual.

Instead of moving away, the Good Samaritan was moved with compassion. He knew that failing to do good was just as bad as doing evil. Therefore, he put the Golden Rule into action. And to that example, Jesus said, "You go, and do likewise." Have you?

HOSPITALITY

A Catholic priest in Bardstown, Kentucky, showed hospitality to a stranger who ended up staying for several months. The stranger did not do anything to help the parish; and when he left, he gave only his thanks. Several years later, some of the most beautiful paintings in the world arrived at the little church. It turns out the stranger was a  prince of France in exile; and when he returned home, sent a royal gift to the priest.

"Hospitality" comes from a Greek word (*philoxenian*) that means "stranger lover." The idea is being generous or kind to guests. It was a highly esteemed virtue in the ancient world and is strongly emphasized in the New Testament. And as the above story demonstrates, we never know just how far reaching a simple act of hospitality might be!

TRADITION

We need to be fashioned after the old, without being old fashioned. While our services should be patterned according to the New Testament, that doesn't mean we have to sit on wooden pews surrounded by stained-glass windows singing hymns from the 1800s. Nor does it mean using archaic language like "thee" and "thine" or wearing fancy suits.

I believe that a failure to distinguish between "truth" and "tradition" has caused some churches to lose touch with modern society and their influence has been marginalized. We must see the difference between commands and customs, precepts and preferences; and recognize that some changes are good!

THE PONY

A set of twin brothers were alike in just about every way. However, there was one noticeable difference. One of the brothers saw the downside in every situation while the other was extremely optimistic. Their parents were concerned about this and consulted a doctor, who suggested that they give the pessimist a new bike and the optimist a box of manure to see how they would respond. When the pessimist saw the bike, he said, "I'll probably crash and break my leg." When the optimist saw the manure, he ran outside screaming, "You can't fool me! Where there is this much manure, there has to be a pony around here somewhere!"

Winston Churchill once said, "I am an optimist. It does not seem too much use being anything else." That is certainly true. And no one has more reason to be optimistic than Christians. Our past is past, our present is a present, and our future is brighter than we could ever imagine. There is no need to mope for those who have hope!

MERCY

A young man had committed a certain offense twice, and Napoleon felt that justice demanded death. When the man's mother begged for mercy, Napoleon said, "Your son does not deserve mercy." "Sir," the woman cried, "it would not be mercy if he deserved it." Napoleon replied, "Well, then, I will have mercy." He spared the man.

While "grace" is getting what you don't deserve, "mercy" is not getting what you do deserve. It is the outward manifestation of compassion or pity. All of us have committed offenses that demand death. That is what we deserve. Yet God has made it possible to receive mercy rather than justice. We must remember, however, that those who receive mercy must give mercy. As James declared, "There will be no mercy for those who have not shown mercy to others…" (2:13, NLT).

FISHERMAN'S FORTUNE

An American tourist complimented a Mexican fisherman on his quality of fish and asked him how long it took to catch them. The fisherman answered, "Not very long." "Then why not stay out longer and catch more?" the tourist asked. The fisherman explained that the small catch was sufficient to meet the needs of his family and allowed him to sleep late, play with his children, and hang out with his friends.

The tourist interrupted, "If you work longer and catch more fish, you can buy a bigger boat and catch even more fish. With the extra money, you can get an entire fleet and start selling directly to processing plants. You can leave this little village and move to New York and run your business from there." The fisherman wondered, "How long would that take?" "Probably twenty years," the tourist replied. "And after that?" asked the fisherman. "Then you'll be able to retire and move to a small village near the sea, where you can sleep late, fish a little, play with your grandchildren, and hang out with your friends."

OUR HERO

In December of 2012, members of SEAL Team Six travelled to a Taliban compound where an American doctor was being held hostage. One of the SEALs, Edward Byers, subdued a Taliban captor and then flung himself on top of the doctor to shield him from gunfire while pinning a second Taliban captor to the wall. He was awarded the Medal of Honor for his heroic actions.

The heroic actions of Edward Byers are admirable. He put his life on the line to save someone else. They are also reminiscent of another example of self-sacrifice. Because we were being held hostage to sin, Jesus travelled to earth, subdued our captor, shielded us from harm by putting His life on the line, and was awarded the highest honors by God the Father. Jesus sacrificed Himself "to rescue us" (Galatians 1:4)!

POSSESSED BY POSSESSIONS

An elderly man was about to die and thought he had figured out a way to take his money with him. He told his wife to put all his money in a bag in the attic above his bed, so he could grab it on the way up to heaven. Shortly after he passed, his wife went into the attic and saw the bag still sitting there. "That old fool," she chuckled. "I told him to put the money in the basement!"

We have all heard the expression, "You can't take it with you," but that hasn't kept some people from trying. For instance, a 90-year-old South Carolina man was buried in his prized 1973 Pontiac Catalina along with his gun collection because he didn't want to leave this world without them. Yet Solomon tells us that such effort is foolishness, for "we all come to the end of our lives as naked and empty-handed as on  the day we were born. We can't take our riches with us" (Ecclesiastes 5:15). Rather than being possessed by possessions, let's get busy storing up the treasures that really do last... the heavenly kind!

THANKFULNESS

Matthew Henry (1662-1714) was once robbed of his wallet. Knowing that it was his duty to give thanks in all things, he mediated on the incident and then wrote this in his diary: "Let me be thankful, first, because he never robbed me before; second, because although he took my purse, he did not take my life; third, because he took all I possessed, it was not much; and fourth, because it was I who was robbed, not I who robbed."

"Thankfulness" should be one of the most obvious differences between those who follow Christ and those of the world. Rather than dwelling on the negative, Christians focus on the positive and find reasons to rejoice. We look for the good in all circumstances, even when they are hard to find.

WHERE'S YOUR HEART?

David Livingstone was a Scottish missionary in the nineteenth century. He went to Africa and spent many years working among the tribes there, until he contracted a disease and died on May 1, 1873. The people sent his body back to England for proper burial but cut out his heart and buried it in African soil before doing so. They said, "You can have his body, but his heart belongs in Africa!"

Where would your heart be buried? Would it be buried at the office? At the ballgame? At the bar? At the lake? At the mall? This is an important thought to ponder, for the Lord once said, "Where your treasure is, there your heart will be also" (Matthew 6:21).

SACRIFICE

A pig and a chicken were walking through the poor section of a city. The chicken said to the pig, "Look at all these hungry people. Let's give them some ham and eggs for breakfast." The pig replied, "Wait a minute! For you, it's a donation. For me, it's a sacrifice." When you give to the church, are you just making a donation to the Lord or are you really sacrificing to the Lord?

The widow's offering of two small coins was of far less monetary value in Luke 21, yet Jesus said she gave more than them all. Do you know why? Because they had given of their "surplus," but she had given "everything she has." — *Donation Versus Sacrifice!*

COMPROMISE

A hunter was about to shoot a bear in the woods. Just before he pulled the trigger, the bear asked, "What is it you want?" The man replied, "I want a fur coat for the winter." The bear then said, "And I want a full stomach. Let's compromise." Later, the bear got up and walked away alone. He had his full stomach and the hunter had his fur coat.

That is a good illustration of how it is with spiritual compromise. It is always one-sided. Though it may seem reasonable at the time, it ends up taking you further and costing you more than intended. And in the end, the devil is the only one who leaves satisfied!

WOUNDED STRANGERS

Four Navy SEAL commandos were on a mission in Afghanistan in 2005 when they encountered Taliban fighters. Three of the commandos were killed. The fourth was severely injured but was able to crawl seven miles through the mountains before he was taken in by a Pashtun tribe. The tribe took the wounded stranger in, supplied his needs, and risked everything to protect him from the Taliban fighters until there was no one left.

There was a time when we were all wounded and wearied crawling aimlessly through the mountains of life with the enemy on our tail, and yet God graciously welcomed us into His home, cared for us, and sacrificed everything to keep us from harm. He did for us what we could not have done for ourselves!

PATIENCE

Edwin Stanton was a ruthless rival of Abraham Lincoln. He went so far as to call Lincoln "the original gorilla" and a "low cunning clown." Lincoln did not reply to his personal attacks and later named Stanton to be his war minister, all the while treating Stanton with courtesy. After Lincoln was shot in the theater, Stanton went to the

president's side with tears in his eyes and declared, "There lies the greatest ruler of men the world has ever seen." Patience prevailed!

"Patience" is the ability to stay calm when provoked and to endure injury without retaliating. It is a noble quality that is repeatedly emphasized in the New Testament. It is a characteristic of love (1 Corinthians 13:4), it is a fruit of the Spirit (Galatians 5:22), it is part of the Christian's walk (Ephesians 4:1-2) and it is part of the Christian's wardrobe (Colossians 3:12).

FORGIVENESS

It took Thomas Edison and his men 24 straight hours to make just one light bulb. When Edison finished making one of them, he gave it to a young man to carry up the stairs. Step by step he cautiously watched his hands, terrified of dropping such a priceless piece of work. At the top of the stairs, the young man dropped the bulb. The team had to work 24 more hours to make another one. When they finally finished, Edison gave the bulb to the same young man to carry again.

Forgiveness, which comes from a Greek word that means "to send from," is the pardon of an offense as if it never occurred. It is let go. It is not held over their head or placed on standby for use later. The hatchet is buried, and not with the handle sticking out of the ground!

SAUL OF TERROR

It's late at night. There's an eerie silence on the empty street outside. A small group of disciples is huddled together in a room somewhere near Damascus. The only light comes from a flickering flame in the corner. They are praying for their brothers and sisters in Jerusalem who have been repeatedly attacked by a blood-thirsty terrorist named Saul. He hit six houses on his last raid, carrying off men and women to prison. And to make matters worse, they hear he's headed their way.

The conversion of Saul is one of the most remarkable stories in the Bible. He was the last person you would expect to become a Christian. After all, he was part of the murderous mob that stoned Stephen to death, led a spiritual SWAT team into private residences to arrest disciples, and voted for the death penalty when they went on trial. If anyone was "too far gone" it was the saint-slayer from Tarsus! Yet God turned his mess into a message. And he can do the same for you!

ANTS IN YOUR PANTS

Paul Railton of Consett, England, was fined and barred from driving for six months after a cyclist witnessed him "walking" his dog while driving. Railton was holding the leash out the car window as he drove slowly down the street. Though he pled guilty to the charge of "not being in proper control of a vehicle," the real crime was laziness.

The lazy person asks someone else to change the channel, walks by an overflowing trash can without emptying it, drinks straight from the milk carton, coughs without covering his mouth, daydreams with a deadline approaching, doesn't flush the toilet, never uses a blinker, hides from the boss, and arrives late to appoint-

ments. He is stuck in neutral and has no drive in his life. — The lazy person needs to get some "ants in his pants" (Proverbs 6:6-11)!

MILK

A young man named Howard Kelly was selling goods in a neighborhood to pay his way through school. When he came to a certain house and was feeling fatigued, a young lady gave him a glass of milk. He offered to pay for the milk, but she replied, "You don't owe me anything. My mother taught me to never accept payment for kindness."

Years later, Dr. Howard Kelly was asked to help with a woman who was critically ill. When he heard the name of the small town where she was from, he immediately went to her room in the hospital. He recognized his new patient at once. She was the kind milk-giver! Kelly gave special attention to her case and after a long battle she got better. Then he paid off her medical bills and sent a note that said, "Paid in full with one glass of milk!"

ARE WE THERE YET?

"Are we there yet?" That is an all-too-familiar question on many road trips. You know it's coming when the kids start growing restless in the backseat. They can't get comfortable. They can't get along with one another. They can't get why dad has to sing along to the radio. It is an irritating inquiry from an irritated inquirer and once the words come out, they tend to reappear.

Though she may not have verbalized it, I can imagine that Mary probably felt like asking that question on the long trip from Nazareth to Bethlehem. After all, it was about an 80-mile journey over bumpy and hilly terrain, she was riding on a donkey, and she was pregnant. Nine months pregnant! If anybody had a right to cry out "Are we there yet?" it was Mary.

THE COMMA

Alexander III was the emperor of Russia from 1881-1894. On one occasion, he signed an order consigning a prisoner to life in exile. It read simply, "Pardon impossible, to be sent to Siberia." His wife Maria, however, was very compassionate and when she saw the order, did something that would change the prisoner's life in a big way. She moved the comma. It now read, "Pardon, impossible to be sent to Siberia."

All of us were guilty of sin and should have been eternally exiled. Yet God made pardon possible through His Son. Jesus left the glories of heaven to die as a perfect sacrifice so we could have the comma changed from "Pardon impossible, to be sent to Siberia" to "Pardon, impossible to be sent to Siberia."

JUST ASK

Governor Mike Beebe of Arkansas made headlines when he announced plans to pardon his son, who had been convicted of felony marijuana possession years earlier. Some agreed with the governor while others criticized him, but what stuck out to me was his comment to a Little Rock television station. Beebe said, "I would have done it a long time ago if he'd have asked, but he took his sweet time about asking."

I imagine the father of the prodigal son would have said the same thing in Luke 15. If asked why he put the robe, ring, and shoes on his son and had the fattened calf killed for a celebration dinner, he would have probably said, "I would have done it a long time ago had he returned, but he took his sweet time about returning."

BROTHERLY STUFF

Rodney Gilliam stabbed his brother Randy repeatedly with a three-pronged fork during a dispute over pot roast. Randy was left with stitches, a swollen eye, and a busted lip. He brushed off the situation as "brotherly stuff."

When strife arose between Abram's herdsmen and Lot's herdsmen, the patriarch defused the situation and deferred to his nephew for one simple reason — "we are brothers" (Genesis 13:8); and when Moses saw two Hebrews fighting amongst themselves, he sought to reconcile them for the same reason — "you are brothers" (Acts 7:26). Obviously, Abram and Moses understood the importance of brotherhood. They knew that "being brothers" outweighed "being bothered," and acted accordingly. Christians should do the same!

MARY

Mary just did not fit the profile. She was the exact opposite of what you would expect. Everything about her situation seemed to defy conventional wisdom and push the bounds of reason. After all, she was an unwed teen with no child-rearing experience or social standing. She was not a princess, but a peasant; not the wife of a king, but the girlfriend of a carpenter; not Jerusalem's jewel, but Nazareth's nobody. Who would have thought?

Out of all the women God could have chosen to be the earthly mother of Jesus, He chose Mary. She was the one who would fulfill Isaiah's prophecy uttered hundreds of years earlier, "Behold, the virgin shall conceive and bear a son, and shall call his name Immanuel" (Isaiah 7:14). Yet another example of God's extraordinary use of ordinary people. You don't have to be impressive to leave an impression!

DON'T STAND DOWN

Dakota Meyer, a United States Marine, heroically rescued 36 people during an intense battle in Afghanistan. He defied orders to stay back and made five trips into the kill zone under constant gunfire to save others.

As a result, Meyer was awarded the Medal of Honor by President Obama on September 15, 2011.

Meyer's defiant determination is to be commended. He answered to a higher calling that day, putting his own life on the line in the process. It reminds me of the defiant determination of Daniel, who kept on praying, and of Peter, who kept on preaching. It is also reminiscent of the Hebrew midwives, Shiphrah and Puah, who defied Pharaoh's orders and kept on preserving the life of baby boys. They all had the courage to "stand up" when told to "stand down."

POTENTIAL

When Jesus met Simon, He looked at him intently and said, "You shall be called Cephas," or Peter ("rock"). This name change was due to the potential Jesus saw in him. He looked beyond what Simon was to what Simon could become.

Reaching Simon's potential was not easy. He made plenty of mistakes. He tended to be impulsive and undisciplined at times. However, he finally lived up to his new name. He became a "rock" for the Lord. In Peter, we see that there is no limit to our capabilities if we don't "cap" our "abilities."

YOU DON'T EARN IT

Grace can be hard to comprehend in our world of earning. We are used to students earning their grades, scouts earning their badges, players earning their positions, soldiers earning their ranks, and workers earning their paychecks. It is all about getting what is "rightfully yours" based on some form of achievement. That is the opposite of grace. It is not merit-based, but mercy-based.

This is not to say that obedience is unnecessary. Jesus declared, "Not everyone who says to me, 'Lord, Lord,' will enter the kingdom of heaven, but the one who does the will of my Father who is in heaven" (Matthew 7:21). John added, "...whoever does not obey the Son shall not see life, but the wrath of God remains on him" (John 3:36). There are many other passages that make the same point. We must be obedient to please God. However, our obedience constitutes a yearning, not an earning. We are calling out, not cashing in. We should never trust that our own actions merit salvation.

PARDON

In 1830, a man named George Wilson was sentenced to death by hanging for mail theft. President Andrew Jackson gave Wilson a pardon, but he refused to accept it. This puzzled the authorities who did not know whether Wilson should be freed or hanged. Finally, the Supreme Court ruled that a pardon is an act of grace which must be received to be completed. Without that acceptance, it is of no effect. Therefore, George Wilson was ordered to be hanged.

All of us have sinned and fallen short of God's glory. The sentence for this crime is eternal death. Yet Jesus Christ came to earth, lived a perfect life, and was sacrificed on the cross so we could be pardoned. It is being freely offered as an act of grace. However, we must accept the pardon for it to be completed. We do that through an obedient faith (Romans 6:17-18).

LEGACY

In 1888, Alfred Nobel was astonished to see his own obituary in a French newspaper with the headline: "The Merchant of Death is Dead." It went on to say, "Dr. Alfred Nobel, who became rich by finding ways to kill more people faster than ever before, died yesterday." The paper had confused Alfred for his brother, Ludvig, who had just passed away.

After reading the mistaken obituary, Alfred Nobel became very apprehensive about how he would be remembered and decided to make some drastic changes. He updated his will and specified that most of his fortune, worth about 250 million US dollars, was to be used to create a series of prizes for those who confer "the greatest benefit on mankind" in five areas, including peace. Alfred wrote, "I was so shocked by people's perception that I committed the rest of my life to work toward world peace." — So, what will your legacy be?

WRONG WAY

An elderly woman called her husband as he was driving home and said, "Herman, I just heard on the news that there's a car going the wrong way on Interstate 90. Please be careful!" Herman replied, "It's not just one car, there's hundreds of them!"

It is easy to travel through life assuming we are right and everybody else is wrong. This is especially true in matters of religion. We feel like others have the problem, not us. We don't need to change course, they do. May God help us all to stay humble in our continuing search for truth.

DON'T MISS THE BOAT

A preacher got swept out into the ocean and couldn't swim. When a boat came by, the captain yelled, "Do you need help, sir?" The preacher replied, "No, God will save me." A little bit later, another boat came by and a fisherman asked, "Hey, do you need some help?" The preacher replied again, "No, God will save me." Eventually the preacher died and found himself standing before God. He asked, "Why didn't you save me?" God answered, "You fool, I sent two boats!"

That's kind of how it works with us sometimes. We trust in God to help but fail to see His hand in the opportunities that come our way. For instance, we pray that God will send honest hearts into our lives to teach, yet never consider that it just might be the annoying trainee forced on us at work. — May God help us to see His hand in the boats that come along!

HATS

"Are We Done Yet?" is a movie about a man who moves his wife and her two kids to the country. Chuck Mitchell is the local realtor who sells them their new home. He then shows up as the local contractor and later as a city inspector. In each role, Chuck takes on a seemingly new personality. When Chuck shows up as the contractor and is asked why the house's problems weren't mentioned earlier, he replies, "In all fairness, I did have my realtor's cap on… My contractor's hat was safely at home in the closet."

Sadly, I think some Christians are like Chuck. They have a collection of "hats" that determine who they are and how they behave. Each one brings out a new personality. When wearing their spiritual hat on Sunday morning, they are kind and prayerful. When wearing their entertainment hat on Friday night, they are wild and worldly. Their hat determines their heart! Could that be true of me?

RANSOM

Paul Jennings was a slave of President James Madison and his wife Dolley Madison. Dolley later sold Jennings to an insurance agent named Pollard Webb for $200. The next year, Daniel Webster paid $120 to purchase Jennings' freedom.

Daniel Webster paid the price for Jennings to be set free from physical slavery. Jesus Christ paid the price for all of us to be set free from spiritual slavery. He gave Himself as a "ransom" (Matthew 20:28; 1 Timothy 2:6), purchasing our release with His own precious blood (Revelation 5:9)!

GETHSEMANE

It was a chilly night in Judea. After eating the Passover in an upper room at Jerusalem, Jesus and His disciples went to one of their favorite hangouts. It was a garden on the Mount of Olives called "Gethsemane." On this particular evening, however, the mood was much more somber than usual. Their place to de-stress became a place of distress.

Jesus took His inner circle — Peter, James, and John — into the inner grove. He was now experiencing overwhelming anguish. His agony was so intense that an angel appeared to strengthen Him and His sweat "became like great drops of blood falling to the ground" (Luke 22:44). The trauma felt by Jesus that night reminds us that His suffering started before He was scourged and crucified. Golgotha's grip was already being felt in the garden of grief!

HOLINESS

There is a small animal called the "ermine" that lives in the forests of northern Europe and Asia. He is known for having snow-white fur in winter, which he instinctively protects against anything that would soil it.

Fur-hunters take advantage of this unusual trait of the ermine. Rather than setting a trap to catch him, they will instead find his home and smear the entrance with grime. Then they set their dogs loose to find him. The frightened animal flees toward home but doesn't enter because of the filth. Rather than soil his white coat, he stays outside until he is eventually captured. For the ermine, purity is more precious than life. And that's the mindset Christians are to have as those who have been set apart from the world unto God. That's the mindset of holiness!

SELFISH DESIRE

On December 3, 1979, thousands of young people stood outside of Riverfront Coliseum in Cincinnati, waiting for *The Who* concert that evening. Seating was on a "first-come, first-served" basis, and when the gates finally opened there was a mad scramble for the best seats. The frantic pushing and shoving caused several to fall, and the result was tragic. Eleven people lost their lives by either being trampled on or suffocated, while eight others were seriously injured.

That incident is a vivid reminder of man's selfish desire. The concert-goers were so intent on having the best seats that they literally stepped on other people to get them. And sadly, such self-interest is prevalent in our society. Some folks are so determined to get ahead that they will "step on" anyone in their way. Whether it's lying, stealing, cheating, manipulating, or undercutting, they do whatever it takes to get what they want with total disregard for others.

KILLER CRAVINGS

To kill wolves, Eskimos coat their knife blade with animal blood and allow it to freeze. Then they add more layers of blood until the blade is completely con-

cealed in a block of frozen blood. When a wolf discovers the block of frozen blood, he starts licking it repeatedly. His craving for the blood is so great that he does not notice the sting of the blade on his tongue, nor does he realize that his insatiable thirst is being satisfied with his own blood. The wolf is trapped, longing for more and more until he drops dead in the snow.

That technique is eerily similar to how sin destroys mankind. It draws us in with something we crave (lust), and strings us along until we are finally consumed by it. As James says, "Everyone is tempted by their own cravings; they are lured away and enticed by them. Once those cravings conceive, they give birth to sin; and when sin grows up, it gives birth to death" (James 1:14-15, CEB).

COMEBACK STORIES

There have been a lot of great "comeback" stories in American sports history. In 1994, the Kentucky Wildcats came back from a 31-point deficit in the second half to beat LSU. *USA Today* named that game the greatest comeback in sports history. My personal favorite is the Buffalo Bills historic rally in the 1993 NFL playoffs. They were down 35-3 in the second half to the Houston

Oilers and ended up winning 41-38. To this day, the game is referred to as "The Comeback."

The greatest "comeback" story of all time, however, was not in the realm of sports. It was in the realm of religion. Jesus Christ appeared to be defeated. He had been scourged, spiked, and speared. His opponents had slapped Him around, beat Him to a pulp, and killed Him on a cross. Then His battered body was sealed shut in a tomb. The eerie silence of Saturday seemed to say it all. And then it happened. Just when it appeared that all was lost, Jesus rose from the dead. Now, that's a comeback!

OLDER SON

The older son argued on merit. He was keeping score. He reminded his father that he had "served" longer and "never disobeyed." Since he had put in more time, exerted more energy, done more good, and been more reliable than his brother, he felt the party should be for him. He earned it!

This begs an important question: Which sin was greater? Was the outward action of the younger son more egregious than the inward attitude of the older son? Are sins of the flesh worse than sins of the heart? The older son was guilty of harboring animosity, jealousy, and pride. He was self-righteous and stubborn. In fact, the only person he could speak to peaceably was the servant. Rather than resenting his father's grace, he should have rejoiced in it!

SHEEP

Have you ever seen a "Beware of Sheep" sign posted on a fence? Probably not. That is because sheep are not dangerous animals. They are weak and vulnerable creatures that often make for easy prey. Sheep don't have speed, sharp teeth, piercing claws, or an intimidating roar. They can't scamper up a tree, burrow under the ground, change colors, or fly away. They are dumb and defenseless.

It is not exactly flattering to be called "sheep." However, it is a fitting analogy. We are like sheep in more ways than we often realize. For instance, we get restless, we tend to wander, we lack direction, we need protection, and we are unable to provide for ourselves. The good news is that Jesus Christ offers to be our shepherd, and with Him by our side we have nothing to fear!

GREAT FISH

The book of Jonah is not very long. It only has 48 verses in four short chapters. However, it reads like a Hollywood movie. A man betrays his boss and goes on the run. He ends up being thrown from a ship into the sea. There is a severe thunderstorm and a giant fish. The fugitive ends up in enemy territory where a dramatic confrontation takes place. And just when you think all is lost, an entire city is saved from the brink of destruction.

The belly of a fish is not a good place to live, but it is a good place to learn. That was true of Jonah and it is true of us. I believe God still sends "fish" to swallow us up from time to time. These fish cause us to slow down and reevaluate ourselves. It might come in the form of a breakup, or a layoff, or a setback. It might be a health scare or a financial crisis. These moments are not comfortable, but they do often serve the purpose of getting us back on track.

THE OTHER JESUS

There were three men on death row that day. They had been convicted of their crimes and sentenced to crucifixion. The crosses they would die upon were already constructed and stored nearby, right next to a bucket full of large nails. The stench of lambs being led to the slaughter was nothing compared to the smell of that fresh cut wood. As the sun rose over Jerusalem, their hearts sank in anticipation of what was coming. Time  was running out and they knew it. One of the men was named Jesus.

The "Jesus" scheduled to be crucified between two thieves that day was not Jesus Christ, it was Jesus Barabbas (Matthew 27:16, NRSV). He was a robber, murderer, and insurrectionist. He was the worst Pilate could offer. Remarkably, the Jesus that ended up being crucified was the best that God could offer. The symbolism is even more impressive when one considers that "Barabbas" means "son of the father." Hence, "Jesus, son of the father" was replaced with "Jesus, Son of the Father." And for that, I am thankful!

ACCENT

When Jesus was arrested and taken before the high priest, Peter lingered in the courtyard to see what would happen. It was there that he denied the Lord three times. The third denial was prompted by this accusation: "Certainly you too are one of them, for your accent betrays you" (Matthew 26:73).

Peter's manner of speech was an indication of his association with Jesus. While I recognize that this text refers to some actual distinction in his pronunciation, there is a spiritual application to be made. Christians should have an accent that gives them away! Just by listening to us, people should be able to tell that we follow Jesus. They should be able to say with the same confidence as Peter's accusers, "Certainly you too are one of them, for your accent betrays you!"

STORM SHELTER

Before a severe storm hit western Pennsylvania, David Kostka was umpiring a little league baseball game. When he saw a black funnel cloud heading toward the field, he rushed into the stands and grabbed his niece. He then pushed her into a nearby ditch and covered her with his body. After the tornado passed, the girl's uncle was gone. He had given his life in the deadly storm to save her life.

Jesus loved us so much that He left heaven, came to this earth, lived a perfect life, and died on the cross to shield us from the devastating effects of the storm of sin. He gave His life to save ours!

PAST

Do you have a past? Most of us do. Perhaps it was a failed marriage, a criminal record, a drug addiction, an attempted suicide, or years of negligence. Maybe it was an affair or an abortion. You know what I'm talking about. It was that time in your life you vowed to forget but always seem to remember. If so, you are not alone. The Samaritan woman at the well had been divorced nearly a half-dozen times and was now living with her boyfriend. This made her a black sheep in the community.

While others tried to avoid this "sinful senorita," as is evidenced by her coming to the well at midday, Jesus engaged her in conversation. He put His own reputation on the line and reached out to the Samaritan woman in spite of her race, her sex, or her sin. She was not too bad or too broken for the Lord. His grace was greater than her disgrace!

GORILLA WARFARE

The gorilla in a zoo was holding a Bible in one hand and a book of evolution in the other. He looked confused, so somebody asked him, "What are you doing?" The gorilla responded, "I am trying to figure out if I am my brother's keeper or my keeper's brother."

Evolution says that about 13.7 billion years ago a tiny singularity (either of matter or energy) exploded, resulting in inflation which led to the material universe. Yet it cannot explain where that tiny singularity came from, what caused the tiny singularity to explode, or how a tiny singularity exploding could produce such a massive effect. All it can do is assert that "might" is right. The Bible, on the other hand, gives a more viable explanation — "In the beginning, God created the heavens and the earth" (Genesis 1:1). That simple verse answers all the questions that evolution cannot answer. Deliberate creation versus spontaneous evolution. Which do you believe?

GEHAZI

Barbara Erni was an eighteenth-century swindler. She concocted a plan that defrauded a lot of people and made her very rich. She would travel the countryside with a trunk that she claimed was full of treasure. Wherever she rested at night, she demanded that her hosts put the trunk in their most secure room available — usually where the valuables were kept. Once the trunk was locked away and everyone went to sleep, a small man would emerge from it and gather everything of worth. Then the two would flee into the night. Though the scheme worked well for Barbara for several years, she was eventually caught and executed. Her luck had run out!

Barbara's story reminds me of Gehazi in the Old Testament. He too concocted a plan to defraud someone of their valuables. Whereas she pretended to be concerned about a chest, he pretended to be concerned about a guest. And like her, his greedy scheme was uncovered and severely punished. His luck ran out!

PERFORMANCE-BASED

We have all been programmed to be performers. Our grades in school are based on performance, our badges in Scouts are based on performance, our positions in sports are based on performance, and our paychecks at work are based on performance. It is all about how good we do. It is no wonder then that some Christians seem to view religion the same way. They think it is performance-based. Having relied on personal achievement for validation in every other aspect of life, they naturally carry that mindset over into spiritual matters.

The Gospel is not about how well we perform for God, it is about how well God performed for us. It is a message of His grace, which means "unmerited favor" or "undeserved blessing." And that's a good thing because none of us can perform good enough to impress God!

COMMUNICATION

A man and woman were driving through Louisville arguing about how it should be pronounced. The man said it should be pronounced "Louie-ville," while the woman said it should be pronounced "Lool-vul." The argument got so heated that they finally pulled over, walked into a restaurant, and said to the lady behind the counter, "Ma'am, could you help us settle a dispute? Please pronounce where we're at very slowly." The lady leaned over and answered, "Burrr-gurrr King."

Communication is crucial when teaching the gospel to others. We can't just assume that they know what we mean. For instance, a person might think that "baptism" is a sprinkling or that "church" is a building or some denomination. We need to clearly define what it is we are talking about.

LYING

A store manager heard his clerk tell a customer, "No, ma'am, we haven't had any for a while and it doesn't look as if we'll be getting any soon." Horrified, the manager came running over to the customer and said, "Of course we'll have some soon. We placed an order last week." Then the manager pulled the clerk aside and snarled, "Never, never, never say we're out of anything. Say we've got it on order and it's coming. Now, what was it she wanted?" the clerk replied, "Rain."

We live in a society where lying is the norm. — Advertisers lie to make money, politicians lie to get elected, lawyers lie to get judgments, employees lie to get promotions, friends lie to get approval, guys lie to get girls. — Leonard Saxe, a polygraph expert and professor, said, "Lying has long been a part of everyday life. We couldn't get through the day without being deceptive." Christians, however, are to be different. We are to "put away falsehood" and "speak the truth" (Ephesians 4:25), knowing that "lying lips are an abomination to the Lord" (Proverbs 12:22).

LORD'S SUPPER

Jesus was on the cross for six hours. Six long hours. — The scorching sun beaming down upon His head (at least for three of those hours); being unable to wipe the sweat and blood from His eyes; the swarming insects landing on His open wounds; the splinters in His back and arms; the dry mouth; the cracked lips; the cramped muscles; the cricked neck; the inability to get a good breath — it's no wonder Cicero referred to crucifixion as the "cruelest and most disgusting penalty."

"Communion," or the Lord's Supper as it is often called, takes our minds back to the day Jesus died. It reminds us of what He endured on the cross for us. As we eat the bread and drink the cup, we reflect on the price Jesus paid in order to redeem man-kind. Whereas the Passover observance helped Israel remember how they were delivered from physical bondage, the Lord's Supper observance helps Christians remember how they were delivered from spiritual bondage. And we are to do this until He returns!

SUPERMAN

Muhammad Ali was on a plane when one of the flight attendants requested that he fasten his seatbelt. Ali audaciously responded, "Superman don't need

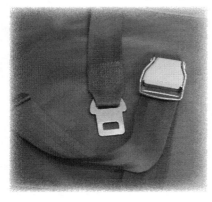

no seatbelt." Without hesitation, the flight attendant replied, "Superman don't need no airplane, either!"

In the Sermon on the Mount, Jesus said, "Blessed are the poor in spirit" (Matthew 5:3). "Poor" does not refer to what a man has, but to what a man is. He knows that regardless of his income or social status, there is nothing to boast about in himself. He is spiritually bankrupt and must trust in God for all things. Ironically, he is the one who will "soar high on wings like eagles" (Isaiah 40:31, NLT)!

THE SHEPHERD

Psalm 23 is undoubtedly one of the most popular passages in the Bible. It appears on pictures, paintings, plaques, and pillows. I have seen it on bumper stickers and billboards, and even tattooed on people's bodies. We sometimes sing it in worship services and often read from it in eulogies. On the night of September 11, 2001, as President George W. Bush addressed the nation from the Oval Office, he quoted from Psalm 23. It is the name of a healthcare agency in Texas and a music store in Florida. And according to *Biblegateway*, Psalm 23 contained four of the top 10 most-popular Bible verses in 2018.

Not only is Psalm 23 a very popular passage, it is also a very powerful passage. David, who had been a keeper of sheep, compares himself to one of those weak, dumb, and defenseless creatures who must rely solely on God for his protection and provisions. And because God is such a strong and trustworthy shepherd, David can confidently say, "I will fear no evil." Hence, it is a psalm of the shepherd's shepherd!

INSTITUTIONALIZED

In the movie "The Shawshank Redemption," a character named "Red" is talking with other inmates about why an old man named "Brooks" doesn't want to be paroled after 50 years in prison. He says it's because Brooks has been institutionalized. "I'm telling you, these walls are funny," Red said. "First, you hate them.  Then you get used to them. Enough time passes and you get so you depend on them. That's institutionalized."

There really is a condition known as "Institutionalization Syndrome," when a person has been incarcerated so long that they cannot function outside of prison. They get so used to a certain system with its rules and regulations that once they're released, they don't know how to handle themselves. This was a problem for Judaizers in the first century, who struggled to live apart from the Old Law; and it is a problem for some Christians today, who struggle to live apart from various traditions. They have come to rely on these walls so much that nothing else seems to make sense.

LIVE CAREFREE

A French philosopher once said, "My life has been filled with terrible misfortune; most of which never happened." I think many of us can relate with that. Studies show that 85% of the things we worry about do not come to pass. — "What if I have a brain freeze and fail the entrance exam?" "What if my son breaks his leg playing football?" "What if my company decides to relocate to another city?" "What if the new neighbors like to party and keep us up at night?" "What if the thing I am worrying about isn't part of the 85%?"

Whereas we tend to worry about things that will not come to pass, Jesus didn't worry about things that would come to pass. Have you ever thought about that? He was still happy and functional, despite knowing that a thorny crown, two cross beams, and three iron nails were in His future. He just trusted in God and lived a carefree life. We are told to do the same (1 Peter 5:7, MSG).

SEDUCING JOSEPH

Have you ever really considered the temptation Joseph overcame at Potiphar's house in Egypt? It was impressive. Here was a young man away from home, he was being hit on by an older woman, she told him exactly how far she was willing to go, she made her advancements day after day, and they were alone in the house.

It would have been easy for Joseph to be seduced by Mrs. Potiphar. Her interest in him was flattering, her position in the home was alluring, and his sexual desires at that age were raging. Yet Joseph refused to sin against God. And though he may have lost his coat, he kept much more — his integrity and standing with God!

EMERGING ALIVE

A forest fire destroyed a farmhouse in western Canada. As the embers cooled, the farmer was walking over the ruins and noticed a burned lump on the ground. It was one of his hens. When he turned the hen over, three chirping baby chicks emerged. The hen saved the lives of her helpless brood at the cost of her own life.

Jesus, who once used a hen analogy Himself (Matthew 23:37), did the same. He laid down His life to save ours. We can emerge from the smoldering ruins of sin because of the Savior's sacrifice for us.

LOSING ITS STING

A man and his young son were driving down a country road when a bumblebee flew in the window. The son was deathly allergic to bee stings and became petrified. Therefore, the man quickly reached out, grabbed the bee, squeezed it in his hand, and then let it go. The boy started to panic again until he saw the stinger lodged in his dad's palm. The man said, "Son, you don't need to be afraid anymore. I've taken the sting out of that bee."

Just as the boy's dad took the sting out of that bee, Christ has taken the sting out of death. He took the pain upon Himself to render it powerless over those He loves. Therefore, we don't have to be afraid anymore. As Paul triumphantly asked, "O death, where is your sting?"